# NOW KNOW

PublishAmerica
Baltimore

First printing

PublishAmerica has allowed this work to remain exactly as the author intended, verbatim, without editorial input.

Softcover 1-60610-649-X
PUBLISHED BY PUBLISHAMERICA, LLLP
www.publishamerica.com
Baltimore

Printed in the United States of America

I dedicate *Now Know* to everyone who is
or was part of my life

with special acknowledgments to

my children and grandchildren

Bill my life long friend

Terrence who saved my life more than once

Those identified within this manuscript

And especially

to Mom

# CHAPTER 1

"Give me a sign. Just make it simple. I'm pretty dumb so make it easy for me to see. If I'm not to do this, GIVE ME A SIGN!"

That's what I said when I was about one third of the way up to where I would make this all go away. I just left Susan my wife of 10 years after she made it very clear to me that she "didn't want to ever have anything to do with me again." She said she was hurt and would never allow herself to go through that pain again. She was right of course, and I accepted the fact that all I did was cause pain to her and the people I love most. It was the last time I ever wanted to hurt anyone again, especially the ones that I love. I left her apartment, barely saying goodbye and headed off to my favorite hike, a relatively easy climb of about 1500 feet to the peak that overlooks most of the valley and beyond. I had not hiked with any consistency for the past few years. It was hiking that pulled me out of my last life crisis over 10 years ago. Now I was going to the place that I had showed my oldest daughter where I wanted my ashes scattered after I passed. It was now where I wanted to be when I passed.

I started off about 4:30 in the afternoon and being late fall there would be another 90 minutes of light at most. My timing was right on. When I would get to the top I most likely would be by myself. Since I was unsuccessful on my first attempt...

*Figuring that 10-12 Codeine tablets with a half a bottle of Brandy would be enough to allow my insurance policies to be cashed in and finally have the ones I love obtain some relief from the hell I had given them over the past few years. With the proceeds Susan could pay back all my friends who believed in me but didn't know of my addiction and especially those who came to my relief and did know. But it didn't work! When I awoke in the late morning of August 5th, I was sick. I was really sick. I could only open my eyes for a second or two at a time. I struggled to a sitting position and then stumbled into the bathroom and vomited a sickly yellow substance. Bent over, I shuffled back to bed and collapsed and gratefully fell back to sleep...*

I was determined to do it right this time. This time I would make sure there would no possibility of surviving or being "saved".

Reaching what I considered halfway marked by two 20-foot saguaro cactuses that a hiker passes between I started to waver. I began thinking about my kids and especially that my youngest son would be in Phoenix for Thanksgiving, just a few days away. I thought of the job that I had just accepted. How it was a perfect fit and feeling that it could be the catalyst to pull me out of my addiction. I started to cry. Again, the pain was upon me. I wanted it to stop. I wanted it to stop forever! I gathered myself and reconfirmed that I was going up the mountain to have the pain go away. I then heard the voice, which I have heard many times before, start a conversation to question if this was the right thing to do...

*I remember hearing voices in my head as a child when I played make-believe but voices that come to me now as an adult are different in that they are not initiated by me. In the early 90's I began a quest to become more than what I was. Praying daily to have me recognize and do the will of God. Now I don't hold the traditional vision of a Supreme Being but one that God is everything. That God is love. There was help in having guidance from the people who came into my life during that time. From an un-healthy state of body, mind and spirit, I grew healthy as I concentrated on thinking and acting on what was necessary to be better. Hiking the desert mountain trails helped me in this transition. All areas of my life improved. With each hike, I was refreshed with the assurance that all is well. I would listen to my internal voice, or should I say, my eternal voice. As I cleared my mind, it would fill up with thought of what needs to be done to reach my goals. One summer evening as I was returning from the peak, I was taken back with the insight I just received. It was the first time, I knew, that this was more then an internal conversation. It was the first time I recognized that I was hearing a voice I recognized as not me. So I asked, "Who are you?" And I heard, "Elijah". "Are you the one that has been filling my mind with my next steps?" I felt his acknowledgement. Then I asked can you give me a sign so that I will know you are who you say you are. The next moment, I was in tears and on my knees for I was given a second or two in viewing of my final judgment. Only I was not being judged by anyone. My judgment was being fully aware of my life and where I failed in being what I am, a child of God.*

I didn't want to hear anything that would intervene with stopping the pain. I stopped listening and reminded myself that death was just a part of life. But I wasn't absolutely sure that this is what I was being directed to do, so again I said, out loud this time: "Give me a sign. I'm pretty dumb, make it obvious."

Deep within me I wanted to stop and turn back and yet I couldn't. I continued up the path refusing to think about what I was about to do and its consequences. I freed my mind by taking in the essence of the desert as I had done hundreds of times before. Many people don't see the beauty of desolation the desert offers. Rocks, scrubby shrubs and cactus are not the usual choice of people who appreciate nature's beauty especially when compared to snow peaked mountains or the ocean seaside, but for me this was home.

It was getting harder now. My knees were feeling the strain of age and lack of use. I started wondering if maybe there could be an alternate location to do myself in. It was getting darker and I was concerned that there wouldn't be enough light to write my goodbye note…no, I should call it what it is…a suicide note. I stopped at a special spot below the saddle between the two peaks. It's where I had a confirmation of my spiritual awakening a few years back, and wondered if this'll do? …The view was OK but it wasn't where I needed to be. It wasn't the view I wanted to see as I would drift into peace. I continued walking.

The sun was below the horizon when I reached my destination. The spot where I wanted to be in my final moments was away from the trail and partially hidden. I sat on a flat rock and took in the view. It was of the north valley where I could see my home, where all my special memories occurred. Breathing in, I placed the instrument of death, a utility knife in a crevice next to me. I smiled as I remembered when I started this hike I left my weapon of choice in my glove compartment and had to stride back to get what I needed to accomplish my goal. Taking another breath and thinking "if you're going to give me a sign it better be soon". With my left hand, I took my notepad from my back pocket and grabbed my pen with my right. I started to write.

"I made it. Out of breath. I love this view. Don't think of this as suicide. If I was seriously ill for 3 years and finally died, you would be happy that I wouldn't have to suffer anymore."

Except when I wrote, "anymore" there was no ink. I tried to free up the ink in the pen by scribbling. Nothing. How was I to leave without letting everyone I love know that my dying was OK? I thought about going to get another pen from the car, and then it dawned on me... THIS IS MY SIGN! I am now speaking with a loud voice... "You gave Moses a burning bush and me; you give a pen that runs out of ink?" I started laughing...and crying. "This is my sign?"

Realizing that I had nothing more to do here, I started my return. It was nearly dark and I was concerned about falling and hurting myself. I laugh every time I think of that. Minutes before, I was *really* going to hurt myself and felt it was a natural act, but now safety was a concern. It truly is amazing how the mind works. I put my "do-myself-in-weapon" back in my pocket along with my pen and notepad, stood up and felt fully aware of everything. I had inklings of this feeling before but this time it was extremely intense. It went through my entire body and I instantly knew that the right decision was made. When I was back on the trail and had gone a short distance, I realized that this day was not yet over. It started with buzzing in my ear and then it became a steady flow of understanding and my acceptance of the many doubts I've been tasked with. Confirmations that my objections to the belief of most people regarding life in the material world was on track.

It was during the first part of the way down that I now grasped that my addiction was not a punishment or a show of dissatisfaction but a gift. In fact, it was one of the greatest of gifts. It was what I had to endure to prepare to fulfill what I agreed to do before I came into this reality.

I was about halfway down when there was a break of the download of understanding. It was then that I questioned my sign. I stated in full voice, "If this is really a sign, the pen will work when I get back to the car." I couldn't help myself in thinking that maybe the pen just ran out of ink.

I continued forward anticipating more downloading to come, but my mind continued that just maybe the pen ran out of ink and there was no sign. Finally, I whispered, "Even if the pen just ran out of ink, I will believe it is my sign." I felt better now and upon releasing my anxiety, the download re-started.

It was dark but for the parking lot lights in the distance when I was about 15 minutes away from the trailhead. I raised my head and continued walking without needing to see where my feet were coming down. It reminded me that modern humans are the only animals that need to look at the ground when walking in nature. I succumbed to my instincts and that let me face the night sky.

I sat down behind the steering wheel and placed the box opener knife back in the glove box. I paused as I reached for my pen and pad. Finally, I pressed the button on the pen top to expose the writing point and scribbled on a clean sheet. I saw the black randomly curved lines on the paper and cried.

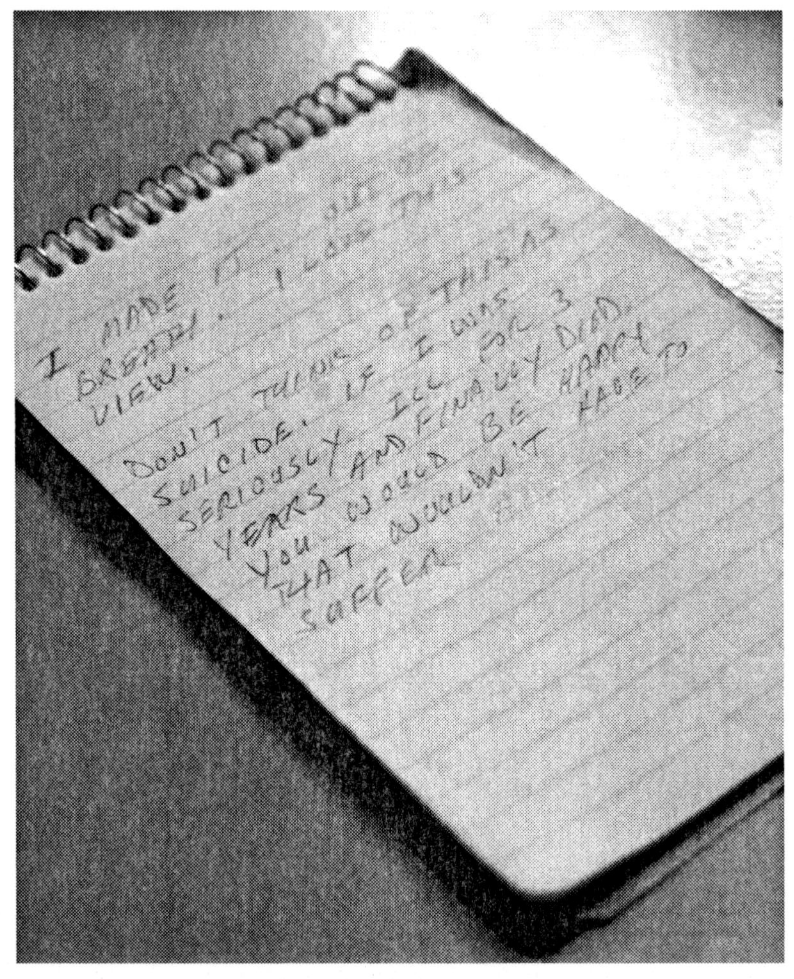


Photo courtesy constantmemories.com

# CHAPTER 2

I was born in Chicago of lower middle class parents right after the end of WWII. My dad would not see me until he was released from the Army when I was almost six months old. My earliest memory was of Bob my older brother by four years, coming home from school. I remember standing on the bench on the stoop of our apartment and jumping up and down while holding onto the back of the bench. My mother doubted my memory until I described it in detail and she responded, "Oh my God that was when we lived on 48th and Paulina". I was two years old.

At five, I had diagnosis of having rheumatic fever. I remember having to go to the doctor's office every day for a week to get shots. My fever went to 105 degrees during that week. When my fever broke, it was decided to have my tonsils out. Moreover, as it turned out my uvula too. This illness had my mother become very protective of me. I was restricted from doing anything physically challenging in fear of my getting ill again and the potential of acquiring rheumatic heart, a condition that took my Uncle Joe's life.

We moved from Chicago's inner south side to the far south side when Mom and Dad bought their first home. I was nine and now had another brother and a sister. Eventually I had three brothers and two sisters. My dad would many times call me "number two", which made me feel second-class since he called my older brother "number one". I was in my thirties when I found out I was "number two" because I was his second child.

My fondest childhood memories include meeting my lifetime best friend Bill; catching tadpoles from the cemetery pond then observe them grow into frogs, feeding the frogs live lightning bugs and watching in amazement how the lightning bug in the frog's stomach would still flash for a minute or so before the bug succumbed; climbing the tree in our front yard and reading all day long; and learning how to play the accordion when I was eleven which was considered old for a beginner.

My teenage years, as for most, were defining. My first day of high school began with a punch in the mouth and because of it; I became a "greaser". I quickly learned it was to one's advantage to pick a fight rather than waiting for one to come to you. But I was an anomaly., Among my peers, I was a hardened attitude laden punk, yet I began teaching accordion to kids 7-9 years old at my accordion teacher's school at 15 where I wasn't a punk but a talented budding musician. My attitude at school cost me when again at 15, I was consistently in the principal's office for fighting to where one day I was issued an ultimatum...

stop fighting or you'll be expelled. But since my grades were all A's and B's the principal soften the ultimatum with an interview with the director of the Diversified Occupations program which provided students an apprenticeship with a trade organization attending a half day at school and a half day on the job where my performance would be graded and credited toward graduation. I was at my first crossroad in my path. I took the job as a printer's apprentice where fortunately the owner was a man of high standards. It was from Ernie that I learned a formidable message. While working late one evening where only I and Ernie were still in the building, Ernie came back to where I was working and held out a brown paper bag and asked "What can I get out of the bag?". I looked at him, thinking his fondness of beer was now speaking but responded some obvious answers, "socks, book, a wristwatch?" He just kept shaking his head until I ran out of answers, waited a moment, turned away, extended the hand that held the bag and loudly pronounced "You can only get out what you put in!" I had no idea what he meant until years later it dawned on me while in college.

I bought a car that year but could not drive it until I turned 16. It was cool to have a car at 16 even if it was a beaten up 8-year-old four-door Plymouth. Nevertheless, Bill and I had used it for many of our first excursions to experience adult life. However, 16 also brought me a challenge that haunted me nearly the rest of my life.

I started playing in my uncle's girlfriend's neighborhood bar on Friday and Saturday nights. I played for tips. One winter weekend night after Christmas, I was getting ready to go to the bar to play, when my father said he wanted me to stay because he and my mom were going out and that I should baby sit. I was angry but did not say anything. When my younger sister got home about 8:30, I left and went straight to the bar to win tips and get compliments. I was completely surprised to see my mom and dad show up at the bar. Dad was also surprised to see me there too. He did not say anything and in fact, he even asked for a request to play his favorite tune "Mack the Knife". They left about a half hour before I did but I made it home before they did and was upstairs getting ready for bed when they came in arguing. Like most children, having my parents argue made me uncomfortable. I listened even though I did not want to. Then a heard a slap and shortly after my mother crying at first and then hearing her lose it and begin screaming at my father. I ran down the stairs and got between them facing my father. I don't remember the words he threw at me. I only remember the intent was to hurt and intimidate. He was warning me to get out of the way. In the mean time, my mother went into their bedroom. My father punched me, knocking me to the ground. He hovered over me having his anger build while I waited for the next blow. By some miracle, my older brother came home and quickly accessed the situation and began talking to our dad to take it easy and gently guided him into the kitchen while looking back at me and mouthing me to hide. I ran up the stairs and at first went under the bed. I waited a few moments and listened to my dad and brother talking. I heard my dad's anger raising and him cursing me for disobeying him. I got out from under the bed, ran into the hall, pulled down the foldable stairs to the attic, ran up the steps and closed them behind me just in time as my father was coming up the stairs to kill me. "Where is that son-of-bitch? I'm going to kill him" Is what I heard from my hiding place. I was shaking with fear as my dad went berserk going from bedroom to bedroom looking for me. The doorbell rang as I heard my brother repeatedly tell my dad that I had left the house. The police entered the house and shouted up the stairs at my dad to come downstairs. This only made my dad angrier and resulted in his semi-charging the police officers. The two officers quickly subdued him. He had handcuffs placed on and was forcibly put in the squad car and taken to jail. My mother did not press charges and my father came home the next day. He never again directly spoke to me until I came home on my first leave from the Marine Corps when I was twenty.

In my senior year, Thom who also worked in the Diversified Occupations program and was the program's banquet committee chair found out that I played the accordion and suggested that I be the entertainment for that year's banquet. At a moment of weakness, I said I would do it. I played just a few pieces and became a hit at the banquet. The school principal, yes the same one who threatened to expel me, attended the banquet and asked me to play at the end-of-the-year school assembly. I said I would without giving it a thought. The school assembly was about two weeks away and almost everyday I struggled with the thought of going to the principal to tell him I changed my mind. Nearly no one knew I played the accordion because I knew the stigma that instrument had with teenagers where rock 'n roll was as Elvis was, the king.

I didn't back down and the day came. As I sat behind the podium waiting for my time to perform, I prepared to be humiliated by my "greaser" peers once they gained the knowledge that I was just a nerdy accordion player. I began to play what I call the "Bull Fight" song, *Espana Cana.* When I finished there was complete silence and then after a few seconds a smattering of applause that kept growing and growing until it was deafening. My peers were giving me a standing ovation, even my close-to-danger peers. The principal tried to get control but quickly gave up and waited until there was a lessening of my peers' appreciation. He looked at me and spoke into the microphone that I would play an encore after he gave the final announcements of the assembly. I never again felt more accepted and appreciated.

Bill and I made a pact to join the military right after high school but after my performance at the school assembly; the senior class counselor suggested I go to college, the

Chicago Musical College, one of the best in the nation. Having no college prep courses, I didn't think I could qualify for college but my counselor encouraged me so I took the entrance exam. To my surprise, Roosevelt University accepted my application but only after scheduling academic remedial courses. Entrance to the musical college wasn't easy either. My knowledge of music was acceptable but I wasn't blessed with the gift of song. When I arrived, the professor stated that he would play eight measures and then he wanted me to sing the eight measures he just played. I told him I couldn't sing and he commented, "Everyone can sing". He then played the eight measures and hit the first note of those eight measures, signaling me to begin singing. I finished singing and waited while the professor slowly turned to me and said, "You're right, you can't sing". Still I was accepted and flourished in the musical college while Bill joined the Air Force.

During my senior year in high school, I met my true first love...Sandy. Even though she was only 17 and I was 19 I proposed marriage and she accepted with the caveat, we would not tell her parents. That fall Sandy went to the University of Illinois and I dropped out of school to work full time to save money to pay for a wedding. In mid-October I got a letter from Sandy saying she still loved me but thought it best we parted ways. I was devastated. That same week, I received notice to have a physical for induction into the military. I was in bed for two days until my father yelled, "Get the hell out of bed!", after he passed my bedroom. It was his way of not breaking the vow of silence towards me.

# CHAPTER 3

It seemed as if I was observing the actions revolving my life rather than being part of those actions. A group of twenty or so were called out by a sergeant and told to move to another room. There we waited while the rest of the draftees were processed. It was now late afternoon and it was a relief to have the sergeant come back into the room. He announced that the men in this room are to be inducted into the Marine Corps, instead of the Army. I didn't hear much of what was being said other than, if we decided to go to the Marines we would fly to San Diego for basic training and if we decided to go to the Army, we would be going to Kansas. It was November 15 and I thought spending the winter in California had to be a good thing.

The next day I was on my first airplane flight to California. What a thrill. After landing in Los Angeles, we were guided to the gate of our connecting flight, which was delayed until 9:00 PM. It was raining in San Diego as we taxied toward the gate. As we entered the terminal, a marine gathered the group of inductees and instructed us to follow him. We walked briskly through the terminal and got into a bus, after the last person was on, the marine slipped behind the steering wheel and we pulled out into traffic for the short drive to the USMC basic training post in San Diego. There was an excitement in our voices as we talked about our trip and what we thought would happen next. The bus stopped. The marine driver got off and in came...the Drill Sergeant. All excitement left us and in its place...fear. I remember hearing the scream of "get on the yellow footprints" over and over again. I was the first to get to the yellow footprints and had the first position, being very sure my feet covered the fading, cracked yellow footprints. I looked up and saw a marine above me on the dock and it was hardly a second when I heard him belt out, "Do you think this is funny!" At first, I didn't realize that he was talking to me. "Get that smile off you face before I rip it off", the marine yelled. This time I knew he was addressing me and I all of a sudden I regretted making the decision to spend the winter in San Diego.

Boot camp was what I expected. Before I turned 12, I watched all the John Wayne films where he played a WWII marine. And I dreamt of being one myself until I saw the Jack Webb movie classic "D.I." which realistically portrayed Marine Corps boot camp. The first morning of boot camp re-enforced my feelings of not wanting to be there when we lined up for our first roll call. We were standing at attention, a position we just learned and the drill instructor was now teaching us how to sound off. "After you hear your name, say loud and clear, *Sir, Private*

*Jones here sir!*" There it was, the drill sergeant barking "Private Anderson!" And hearing down the line, a pretty good sounding "Sir Private Anderson, here sir!" That's when it happened, the drill sergeant came running down the line to be in front of Private Anderson, bent low from the waist to get right up under the chin of Private Anderson and yelled "I can't hear you!" My laughter was a natural reaction, after watching and enjoying the popular situation comedy *Gomer Pyle* where that same scene was at the beginning of each episode. It was the last time I laughed until Boot Camp graduation. That drill instructor's face got red and he literally ran over people in formation to position himself less than an inch from my body. He screamed, "Do you think that's funny private!" and punched me in the body. Then he did it again, and again, and again. Each time his punch would push me back until I was now up against the billet hut. He then turned, got back in front of the platoon and finished roll call. Everyone learned a lesson that day.

Half way through boot camp offers the "boot" a reprieve of sorts; it's when the platoon goes to the rifle range to qualify. Just knowing that after the rifle range, it's all down hill made life easier. A couple of days before going to the rifle range, I caught a cold but didn't ask for or receive any treatment. The morning before we were scheduled to qualify at the rifle range, I had some real trouble breathing while doing the morning calisthenics. The drill sergeant rode me until he finally realized I wasn't a malingerer and signaled the corps man to take me to sick bay. I was examined rather quickly and then given the prognosis. I had pneumonia. The doctor said he was recommending me to stay in the hospital for two to three days. I asked him if I will still be able to go to the rifle range after the hospital stay and he informed me that I would be re-assigned to another platoon. I panicked. I did not want to spend any more time in boot camp than necessary. I begged the doctor to give me some medicine and let me return to my unit. With the doctor's fidgeting, I could tell this was a difficult decision. But he relented and said, "OK, you can return to your unit. I'm ordering light duty for you until I check you when you return from the rifle range." To this day, I know this was a sign in my life.

What is still amazing to me is how everyone subjected to this treatment survived and became a marine. I have never felt better prepared for life than while I was in the Marine Corps. What's funny though, it wasn't life we were preparing for; it was either the enemy or our death.

After boot camp, we went to the Infantry Training Regiment (ITR) where we began doing "John Wayne" stuff, like shooting weapons and "camping". It was there that I met my other lifelong best friend, Ollie. Now that wasn't his real name, but it was given to him because he looked like Oliver Hardy of *Laurel and Hardy* fame. Ollie lived in southern California, so with every liberty, I went home with Ollie for some fun, recreation and sometimes some trouble. His mom treated me, and the other marines coming home with Ollie, like royalty. She was a true American Mom. After our advanced training was completed, Ollie went off to Viet Nam and my orders had me going to Camp Lejeune, North Carolina but not before my first furlough since leaving for boot camp. I was coming home after being away for nearly six months.

As I entered the O'Hara airport terminal, I saw my family waving and my youngest sister and brother running toward me. Lots of "welcome home's" and hugs were given to me, as we moved together through the airport and to my dad's car. My dad didn't say much, letting everyone else ask the hundreds of questions but he did talk to me, directly to me. Mom as usual had a mini feast ready at home; dad offered me a beer even though I was not yet 21. Eventually everyone went to bed and only dad and I sat at the kitchen table. There was now something different yet common between us. Dad's defining life event was his time in the Army during WWII when his unit was involved in the *Battle of the Bulge.* He told the story of taking German prisoners back to the rear a number of times. He also told the story, though rarely, of seeing his friend shot and killed, right in front of him. We now shared a bond that all military men have. We talked for hours, he wanting to know every detail of boot camp, especially the weapons I fired. A week later, I was off to North Carolina.

It was about 4 months afterwards when a call for volunteers occurred. The duty was a secret but everyone knew it was for Viet Nam. I put in my name in along with all of the marines I hung with except one, whose girl friend was pregnant. The irony is that this marine was transferred to Nam and killed before the group that volunteered arrived "in-country". I spent another furlough week at home where the family celebrated my 21st birthday. It was my first surprise birthday party; in fact it was the only surprise party I've had. Being of Polish descent, my dad and my uncles made sure I was never without a beer or a shot in my hands. I don't know how I survived the onslaught.

After a few weeks in Camp Pendleton preparing for our voyage to Viet Nam, we boarded a ship with all our equipment and weighed anchor from the Long Beach dock. We weren't out of port 30 minutes when all the "heads" and the railings were filled with marines…vomiting. By the second day, most of us were OK. A few days later our trip brought us into Pearl Harbor for a couple of hours to bring on supplies and mail. About 10 days later, the troops were granted liberty at Okinawa. Hearing Jingle Bells in Japanese is still a fond memory. As we sailed through the South China Sea, we tangled with a tropical storm that had many of us thinking we may not be getting to Viet Nam. The ship literally bounced and shook with each swell. We arrived at Da Nang with the ship listing to port after taking on some water. I was sent to Chou Li, about 30 miles south of Da Nang. I remember how lush and green the countryside was. I couldn't quite grasp that

I was now in a war zone until that first night when sleeping was taxed because of the on-going artillery fire. From my post, which was a little ways from the edge of the bush, I sat with another marine in a flatbed truck with a 600-gallon fuel tank and waited for our troops to emerge from the bush to get fuel. Boring duty, except for the one time when sniper fire came our way.

Four weeks after arriving in Nam, I was in the field when called back to HQ. When I reported to the C.O. he informed me that my dad had a heart attack and my mother requested my return. I couldn't believe he asked if I wanted to go. When I responded "yes", action was taken immediately. I had about 10 minutes to pack before being on a helicopter headed for Da Nang where I joined a group of men from various branches of service waiting to board a huge C4 airplane. Officers usually were processed first but the sergeant at the desk asked if anyone in the group had emergency leave orders. A sailor and I were first to be processed. It was the smoothest flight ever. The altitude we flew gave us a glimpse of the curvature of the earth as we headed to Japan.

I was in Chicago about 34 hours after leaving Viet Nam. It was mid January and I anticipated cold weather but instead, it was a balmy 50 degrees. I visited dad the next day. He was still under close watch though not in critical care. The weather had started to turn to a more normal condition as we left the hospital, which prompted me to say to my mom, "I hope it snows while I'm here. I haven't seen snow for two years." The next morning there was 8 inches on the ground and no let up in sight. I got my wish and my mother got hers. Dad would be not be able to work for quite a while so there would be no income and there were still four siblings at home. She was distraught in the thought of not being able to pay the bills. Even though I gave her all of my savings, it would run out in about a month. I applied and eventually granted a hardship discharge.

My hardship discharge application was quickly approved. It would take about six weeks before my release from active duty would come about. I was temporally assigned to a Maine Corps reserve unit in North Chicago. It was a job and I made an impression on the Gunny (rank of gunnery sergeant) and the commanding officer because I did what I was asked to do as quickly as possible. The first day I was given an assignment to file paperwork. The Gunny explained to me what was to do and left. I finished in about an hour and reported to him where he was amazed that I had already finished the task. He thought I would take all day to do it. It seems other marines having temporary assignment there, while being mustered out, had the attitude of "nothing can happen to me if I malinger". I was pleased just to be busy.

My release came in a few weeks and the Gunny explained I needed to join a Marine Corps reserve unit within three months or I would be eligible to be called back to active duty. I went back to my old job, bought a car and helped the family get through some rough times but I completely forgot about joining a reserve unit until the day I received a letter by certified mail to report to Camp Pendleton in 30 days for re-assignment. Dad was home but had at least another 60 days before he'd be ready to go back to work, so I called the Gunny to ask for his advice. I promptly replied "yes" when he asked if I could come up to the depot that afternoon. The Gunny welcomed me, took my papers and asked me to wait in the hall as he went in to see the Colonel. I watched as the Gunny explained the situation and the Colonel looked over my orders. The Gunny sat down while the Colonel dialed a number on the phone. There was a brief discussion. The Colonel got up from his chair and they came toward me where the Colonel stated, "I've taken care of this. You'll get notification by mail in a few days." I thanked them both and left.

About a week later, I received my Honorable Discharge.

# CHAPTER 4

After receiving my discharge from the Marine Corps, I quit my factory job and took a job at Continental Bank, at that time the eighth largest bank in the USA, as a municipal bond underwriter salesman trainee. This job was a real opportunity because of my lack of higher education. The Vice President of the department told me on my first day that the decision to hire me was made when I answered the question of "What job security do I expect?" With "I have no expectation of job security, only the belief that if I do a good job, I will have a job."

My first couple of days I was orientated on general banking operations and then transferred to the municipal bond underwriting operations. The "cage" is where the physical bonds are counted and verified for authenticity. Adjacent to the cage were data entry stations and the underwriting partner operations. My assignments included duties in the cage, data entry and finally a couple of days doing underwriting partner operations that I performed so well that I was offered the position of supervisor and never did return to the sales floor.

One morning I received a phone call from the municipal bond department's VP at Chase Manhattan Bank (one of our underwriting partners) that tore into my usually calm demeanor. He was yelling over the phone that we mishandled a $10 million underwriting and this better be fixed ASAP or "my ass is grass." I rushed to the operations desk to look for the paperwork on this transaction and there she was saying hello and murmuring something about "I guess he just doesn't want to talk to me." I found the paperwork and was relieved that the issue was not our doing. I glanced back at this attractive girl, who was now busy doing her work and not noticing me at all. However, I noticed that she had some good-looking legs to go along with a friendly smile and attractive face. I went to her desk, apologized for not responding to her "hello", and explained my situation of being is a hurry to fix a problem. She smiled and said, "that's OK". We introduced ourselves and went back to work.

I found out from my associates in the department that Debbie was a clerk in training for the municipal bond sales department. Being attracted to her but not wanting to show that I was interested, I waited outside the bank every morning to see if I could spot her coming to work. It took a few days but I did see her and "accidently" bumped into her. She smiled as she turned and recognized me. Debbie's smile was remarkable. It made me feel totally at ease. We chatted awhile and agreed to meet for coffee. Coffee led to dating up until she asked me to go home to

Nebraska with her for the Memorial Day weekend. I said yes, but when the day came to go pick her up, I got cold feet and didn't go. She called me and was so disappointed and yet understanding. I never felt more like a jerk. Our relationship was over.

Months later, I was startled that there was someone at my desk telling me that my area was under review and some changes will be taking place. I stomped over to the director of the methods and review department and called him an asshole for messing with my operations. I was angry because for over the past year our transactions more than doubled yet I was able to reduce staff by one and a half men by streamlining operations and eliminating duplicate processes. My manger stood behind me and prevented any reprimand. That same director, promoted to assistant VP, came to me a month later and congratulated me on a job well done. A month or so after that, a supervisor from the methods and review department interviewed me to see if I was interested in a computer programming position. The offer included a reduction in my weekly hours to 35, a 10% increase in pay and IBM school for three months. It took all of second to say yes.

Computers in the late sixties were just beginning to be a necessity for large organizations. They cost millions of dollars but also saved millions. I felt very fortunate to be in an area that looked to be a thing of the future. The computer department was housed in a separate high-rise building from the bank. Two floors held the computers and equipment and another floor was for the programmers and analysts. There was a distinction being a computer programmer/analyst that set us apart from everyone else working for the bank. It was a good feeling. Being separate and somewhat treated as prima donnas, some of us ignored the bank's dress code. We didn't always wear ties and some of us, myself included, grew beards.

One morning the director that I called an asshole joined me in the elevator. He was now a full Vice President of one of the bank's divisions. We both said hello and as he started out the elevator door, he turned toward me and said "standing too far from the razor?" I chuckled and smiled. Before the end of the week, a meeting was called to inform us that we must adhere to the bank's dress code. I knew this was his way of getting even. A couple of bearded ones shaved the next day but many of us did not. The following week, we were again reminded to adhere to the dress code and we had one week to do this or else. I was ready for the "or else" when my friend George reminded me that I had put in an "employee suggestion" while I was with municipal bond underwriting and that it could be a good deal of money. I made many friends at the bank and one of them I met while singing in the bank's Christmas choir was an auditor. I asked him if he could check on whether my suggestion was worth very much. My suggestion was to charge interest on the underwriting partners who did not submit their share of the underwriting (a share was usually millions of dollars) on time. Sometimes the partners who were other banks and brokerages let it slide where the bank was forced to come up with the funds on issue or go into default. I put in the suggestion because of all the extra work it caused me, not because of what it cost the bank. The next day, my auditor friend called and told me to shave my beard. He told me that is was in its third and final review. After the first review, the committee sent it back with the comment that the review was in error because of the amount of money involved. The second review presented an even greater savings. The third review verified the findings of the first two reviews. My auditor friend did not tell me the actual savings amount, only that it was substantial. An accepted employee suggestion award was usually 10% of the annual savings.

The deadline to be clean-shaven had past. I still had my beard and no one called me on it probably because it was Christmas week. After the holiday, my manger called me in and offered to accept my resignation rather than have the bank fire me. I resigned and went to HR for exit processing. The HR person apologized repeatedly and could not believe that with my performance with the bank, I was leaving at the bank's request.

When I made my decision not to succumb to the bank's demand, I also decided to move to California. My older and younger brothers lived in San Francisco so I would have a place to stay. I had a New Year's Eve party to play with my band and planned to leave the day after. When I returned home from the bank I started to pack when I got a call from Debbie saying, "I heard you were leaving the bank and I just wanted to wish you good luck". I was surprised and pleased that she called. We talked some about the circumstances of my leaving and I finally asked her if she had any plans for New Years Eve. She didn't so I asked if she would like to come to our "gig". She turned the offer down and when I asked why, she said, "Because I'll be sitting all alone while you're playing". I rebutted if my sax player's wife would come, would she? She accepted. It was great to see Debbie again and after our gig was over, we went to get some food and talked throughout the night. We walked down to the lakeside to watch the sunrise and then headed to "Maxwell Street" for some browsing and shopping. I asked her to come with me to California. She almost considered it.

I stopped in southern LA on my way to San Francisco to visit with Ollie, my Marine Corps buddy for a few days and then off to the city by the bay. It was the first really quality time I spent with my brothers as an adult. It was here when Tom my younger brother and I began talking about starting a coffee house that would be a place where troubled young people could get help or at least the knowledge of where to get help whether it was drug abuse, child abuse, or just not doing well in school. As the idea grew, we decided to move back to Chicago and start it there because we knew the area better. That was our plan. A couple of days before we departed for the trip home, I received a check for $750 in the mail from Continental Bank. It was the award from my suggestion. I called my auditor friend and asked how did this happen. He said the amount was much less from what was originally decided. The estimated bank savings were the largest savings ever suggested by an employee and it was the first time ever to award an ex-employee. He said the original award amount was $7500 and that the committee was not going to give me any award until my former department manager forced the issue to agree to award something.

Tom and I drove most of the way home in a terrific winter storm. Ice in Oklahoma snow and sleet but we made it. Debbie was looking forward to see me.

It was just a few days before Tom and I started in earnest to find a place to rent as a coffee house in the blue-collar suburban neighborhood of Blue Island. We both drove cabs to have some income. We talked to many local businesses about what we were planning and found it easy to speak to community groups. We spoke of how to get control of the day's teenage issues, mostly drugs use and gang related problems. We invited everyone to participate in how this would work. Optimistically we placed some earnest money to rent a vacant bakery shop, which needed a lot of work, but before we could get started, we were shut down by the fire department. We lost our earnest money and needed to regroup and have financing before we would attempt another try. The acceptance when we first spoke to the community groups now all but disappeared. The underlying mode was "there is no problem now but they would bring it here". I gave up.

Now during this time, Debbie and I were getting to know each other better. After our try for being a community presence, I asked her to marry me. She said no, not now. We went to visit her family in Nebraska and what a family. It was a page out of the book *Cheaper by the Dozen*. Nevertheless, I was able to remember the names of all eleven of Debbie's siblings before we left to come back to Chicago. I asked her to marry me again while we were in Nebraska. She said no, not now. The day came late summer on a Thursday that I decided I would ask Debbie to marry me only one more time and if the answer was "no, not now" I would not ask her again. I picked her up from the bank and after parking in front of her apartment, I ask her to marry me. However, this time she said, "How could I marry you, you don't even have a regular job." Which I said, "Will you marry me if I get a job?" She took a deep breath and said, "Yes". The following Monday I had three jobs. That December we were married.

# CHAPTER 5

Our first year of marriage was a time of adjustment and compromise. In addition, after a few months we began discussing having a family. Debbie was at first reluctant. She wasn't fully confident that she could be a good mom. A few months before Debbie became pregnant; I started experiencing a strange sensation in my hands at work. The job I took after my last proposal to Debbie was as a production factory worker that manufactured metal support beams for hanging ceilings and metal two by fours for commercial buildings. Extremely boring work but when a machine needed adjustments to form the product to specification, I took notice on what the "set-up man" did and eventually began making minor adjustments on my own. It wasn't long before the supervisor had me doing set-up work for machines of other workers. I became an official "set-up man" a month later. Eventually the company created a new position called "engineering liaison" for me. This job had me conferring with engineering in deciding the best method of production for new products. My job had me using a wrench a lot. The sensation I started to feel was a tingling in my hands up my arm and it eventually worsen to where I started dropping my wrench.

My family doctor diagnosis was arthritis, and prescribed aspirin. My symptoms worsened and my family doctor referred me to an arthritis specialist. He confirmed that I had generalized rheumatoid arthritis. It was getting hard to get up in the morning. I was stiff and had to shuffle to the bathroom and run warm water over my hands to get them to move. Once I got going, it was OK, except with the discomfort throughout my body. The specialist tried many treatments and eventually could only offer that I should move to a warmer and dryer climate. Debbie was supportive so that fall when Debbie was a few weeks pregnant we drove to Phoenix, camping along the way, to check it out. We only stayed a couple of days but decided that Phoenix will be our home after the baby arrives.

Summer had arrived and Debbie was now about 8 days past due. She saw the doctor in the morning and he told her that it should happen any time. About 6:30 PM that evening, Debbie had some pizza and felt a little funny afterward. Around 8:00 PM Debbie's water broke. I found myself wanting to calm myself down. My emotions ran from excitement to panic. After I called the doctor, we were off to the hospital. Debbie took good care of herself during her pregnancy and really immersed herself in all the information she could lay her hands on regarding childbirth. She was prepared. We took a Lamaze course and felt we had a good handle on our first-born coming into this world.

When we arrived at Michael Reese hospital (considered one of the best hospitals in the Chicago region), everything went according to plan. Debbie continued to dilate at acceptable intervals and she was able to maintain her composure while dealing with labor pains. Until I think about 9:00 am, labor essentially stopped. The doctors had some concern because the baby was breach but they felt it wasn't a major concern until progress stopped. I remember the doctor coming into the room and explaining that they will be looking into options of what to do, one was to induce labor.

We waited maybe an hour when the doctor came in and said they thought it would be in the baby's best interest to perform a C-section. Debbie and I were a little stunned because a natural birth was always the plan. My biggest disappointment was I was not going to be able to participate in the birth. In the early 70's, having a husband participate in a birth was radical. So I went off to the waiting room for what seemed forever, finally the doctor came in and said, "You have a daughter". I went to see Debbie, now a mom, while she was still in recovery. She was cold and though conscious was still not completely coherent. I hugged her and left to see my daughter. I could only see my daughter and not hold her because of the trauma experienced during birth. The umbilical cord wrapped around the baby's neck three times was the reason of not having a natural delivery. Debbie and I picked Jennifer or Constance if it was a girl. When I first saw my daughter, I saw "Constance". Joy became Constance's middle name because that is what Debbie felt when seeing Constance the first time. I left the hospital late afternoon the next day. Bewildered that I was now a father but overjoyed in that fact. Six weeks later, the doctor checked Debbie and Connie, our U-Haul was packed and we were off to Arizona.

I took the first job offered. It was with a small engineering and software company. The pay wasn't very much but I was getting back into computer programming. I was there for about six weeks when my application for a programmer position for the State of Arizona's Revenue department was accepted. I really enjoyed my job and I made a good impression with my boss, Bob who was a partner in the business. When I tendered my resignation, he asked why and I told him that the pay at the state job was nearly double from what I was making there. Bob smiled and said, "You should have told me, I would've paid you that." During my time working at the state office, Bob would call me periodically to see how I was doing and if I'd be interested in coming back to work for him. When he called in January about 16 months after I left, I was ready for a change and besides, he was now offering me more pay that what the State paid me. I did inform Bob that our second child was due in about 4 weeks, and he said, "We'll work around that." I went off to my new job feeling good how things had progressed. Next week Constance will have a brother or sister.

Because Debbie had a C-section for Constance, this baby delivery would also be by C-section. So on the date scheduled by the doctor which was a few days before Debbie's estimated due date, Constance stayed with friends and we were off to the hospital. Again, I was in the waiting room while our second child came into this world. I saw the nurse with a huge smile coming toward me. She stopped in front me and held out our baby saying, "It's a girl." As I held this beautiful squirming little being, I whispered "Jessica". As with Constance, we had a couple of names picked out and for Jessica, the other name was Jennifer. We liked them both very much, so Jessica became the beautiful flowing Jessica Jennifer. After staying a scant two days in the hospital, Debbie insisted on coming home because of the poor service from the hospital staff.

The second day home, Debbie started to run a high fever from an infection around the C-section incision. The doctor prescribed an antibiotic and scheduled a visit in two days. That day Constance was also not feeling well and by nightfall, she had a fever that rose to 104 degrees. When I called the doctor, I received instructions to give her children's Tylenol and a cold bath to bring down her temperature. As the cold water ran into the tub, I undressed Constance and began to let her into the water, the minute her toes touched the water, she screamed. I immediately redrew her from the bathtub and she quieted. I couldn't place her into the water again yet her temperature needed to come down and fast. I slipped off my jeans and while holding Constance, stepped into the water. It was cold! I gently placed Constance between my knees and she was fine. I gently moved water from my palm onto her back and chest. Whenever she squirmed, I spoke gently to calm her. I could feel her temperature was lowering after ten minutes in the bathtub. I was relieved when after we stepped out of the cold water and I took Constance's temperature it was down to 100 degrees. I checked on Debbie who fed Jessica and finally I went to bed.

The next morning, I called Bob to tell him I was not going to be able to come into the office again. I didn't realize it then but now as I look back, Bob knew I needed a break from this stressful time. He offered to arrange for someone to look after Debbie and the girls while I come into the office that afternoon. Just before noon, Zell, Bob's wife, was at my front door introducing her self and swooshing me out the door to get to the office. She was there in the morning for the next two days.

# CHAPTER 6

Bob asked me to put together a cost estimate for a major project to computerize a bulk fuel loading operation for an independent oil company in Indiana. It was more complex than most of the jobs I worked on in the past so I gave extra diligence to develop an accurate and insightful estimate. The senior analyst was also to submit an estimate. The company was awarded the project with the senior analyst's estimate and he became the project manager. Soon after the project began, I was asked to sit in on the development meetings mostly for backup purposes in the event of an unforeseen event. After having a number of meetings, it was apparent to me that the assigned analyst wasn't quite up to the task at hand and eventually senior management noticed that also. I was asked to take over the project, which I accepted even though my work schedule was extremely full even with working about fifty hours a week. I adjusted and re-prioritized my projects and bumped my workweek to about sixty hours a week. I asked management for help on this major project but was told to do the best I could do. I missed a number of benchmarks, to where the client started to apply some "heat". An ultimatum was given in December to reach a certain benchmark by the first of the year. I did what I could do but knew I wasn't going to be able to have the benchmark ready by the first of the year. It was four days before Christmas when Bob called me in his office and stated that I would need to work the Christmas holidays in an attempt to have the benchmark ready by the designated time. I refused saying I have two kids at home where Christmas is the best of times. I had to be there for them. Bob hinted what the decision would need to be if I refused and told me to take the rest of the day off and think about it.

"What are you doing home?" Debbie asked as I walked in the door, sensing that something was wrong. I didn't quite know what to tell her and didn't have the opportunity because the girls grabbed my hands and pulled me into the living room which was transformed into a dance theatre. "Daddy sit down and watch us dance," they giggled. They were wearing long flowing dresses that Debbie made them. Debbie joined me and the performance began. After dinner and after the girls went to bed, Debbie and I talked. She was pregnant again, due in March, so having a potentially uncertain future was trying. She listened and confirmed that whatever decision I made she would support it.

I came in the next day, handed Bob my office keys and company credit card, and resigned immediately. Bob was apologetic and thanked me for all I have done for the company during my time there. We shook hands and I started out the door when Bob asked, "Do you have anything lined up?" I walked back into the room laughing, "of course not". Picking up a manila envelope and handing it to me he said, "Well, would you mind looking this project over and give me a bid?" I stood there dumbfounded while he continued, "If we accept your bid, any on-sight work will need to done on off hours, you know, after 5:00 weekdays or weekends. Is that OK?" I shook my head in disbelief and said, "I'll get this back to you tomorrow." Smiling, Bob said, "No, enjoy your holidays and have a bid ready after the first of the year." I received my first contract as an independent consultant to start the New Year right. This was the start of the best of times. Not only was I making nearly double as what my salary was as an employee but I was able to work at home about 50% of the time. I was there to see my kids grow up. Oh, and by the way, my termination became the reason to re-negotiate the contract… "Our project manager quit so…" The client principles involved responded, "We were wondering when the contract would be redone because you were so far below all the other bids." As it turned out, the contract when completed was within 5% of my original bid.

"I had a dream that the baby will be born naturally," Debbie said as she rolled over and kissed me good morning. My response was, "What?" "I'm seeing the doctor Thursday and I'll talk to him about it". I accepted her comment knowing the doctor would talk her out of such a crazy notion. When she returned from her doctor's appointment she said, "The doctor said he'll consider it but you and I will need to discuss this with him next week." Debbie's doctor was recommended by a friend who is a registered nurse and she thought he was the best in Arizona so when we met I was feeling that we were in good hands not at all like the doctor who delivered Jessica. We talked and discussed that having a natural childbirth after a women has a C-section is risky but after having two C-sections it was rarely if ever considered by the medical profession. I was assured that I would finally be able to participate in the birth as Debbie's Lamaze coach. He asked Debbie to leave the room to talk to me alone. The mood changed from informative to serious. He leaned toward me and said, "If a complication happens, our attention will be on saving the mother. If this happens, you will need to leave the delivery room immediately. The anesthesiologist is normally at the position you will be. Do you have any questions?" I didn't. I was scared. I could not grasp why Debbie had to do this but I accepted it.

Debbie was great doing labor as she did with Constance. When dilatation reached the point for delivery, off we went with me in this funny costume of a blue-green gown, shower cap and cloth slippers to the delivery home. Because of the circumstances there was a buzz in the hospital staff knowing that there may be some history making here, well at least an article in the medical journals. I was watching my brave Debbie give birth to our child for the first time. His head first appeared. Then Debbie gave that final push and out he came. "It's a boy," said the nurse. Anthony would become Chip as in "chip off the old block" and William was for Bill my childhood best friend. The nurse brought Chip to me to hold. He looked directly at me. I felt honored to be in his presence, knowing that moment he knew the essence of the universe and God's love. I laid him on Debbie's bosom. We now have a son.

My consulting business had its up and downs, thankfully mostly ups. Nevertheless, I did have periods of employment specifically with an organization that offered one of the first microprocessor small business computers. This product was a fascination but also a path to the future. I wrote application software as well as being the customer services manager for the office in Phoenix and eventually for the Los Angeles and Denver offices. After a confrontation with management regarding discrepancies in pricing and customer service, I resigned right after the first of the year. Similarly, upon leaving a company where I was previously employed, I was offered a contract. Actually, it was a partnership to have my soon-to-be ex-employer share 50/50 ownership with me of a software package for the moving and storage industry. My contribution was to complete writing the software for a client in Denver and support any marketing effort. So again, I began an unsecured future with moving into a new house just two months earlier and having our fourth baby due in just 6 weeks.

Debbie wanted to have one more child. She specifically wanted another boy because then "everyone would have a brother and everyone would have a sister". Perfect logic but how were we to have a boy. Doing quite a bit of research, Debbie found a method that during conception could give a better percentage of the baby being a boy or girl depending on the method used. We practiced the "boy" method and finally Debbie became pregnant. As with Chip the risks involved stayed the same, maybe a little more risky because this would be the second natural childbirth and Debbie was a little older. Well labor came and went. Labor stopped at the dilation point that Constance's labor stopped. There was some drama in the doctor proposing to induce labor. We heard the risks and Debbie accepted the risks in deciding a natural birth is what she wanted. The labor pains intensified but again Debbie handled it. As we headed to the delivery room, Debbie spoke to our son, Joseph Konat. Debbie named the baby very early in the pregnancy because she knew it was a boy. We also discovered during the pregnancy that the method Debbie used to help gender selection was what was to be used to have a girl but that did not deter her in her belief. Being part of a birth again was just as thrilling, first the head, then the body and then the nurse proclaiming, "It's a boy". Joseph was in my arms after being cleaned and weighed. He was more fascinated about his surroundings then my face but now "everyone has a brother and everyone has a sister".

Later that year my father passed away. A few months later, I had contracted Valley Fever. I was attending a moving and storage convention in Las Vegas to see what the competition offered against my software package that was in the final stages of development. I drove there with a demo system. I couldn't afford a booth but I thought the opportunity might be there to show the package's features in my room. I felt peaked one night and went to bed early instead of mingling with the industry's managers and owners. I woke in the middle of the night with welts all over my body. I called the emergency room and got the "take two aspirin and see me in the morning" routine. I called Debbie very early the next morning and asked her to contact our family doctor. When she called me back, the doctor knew what I contracted and said I should see him that day. I packed and drove home stopping only for gas. The doctored examined me and confirmed his earlier diagnosis. By this time, I was feeling very ill. I did get a prescription to help the pain but it didn't help. Later that night I became extremely cold. I literally was shaking so hard, my teeth were chattering. Debbie contacted the doctor. After hanging up the phone, she started to draw a bath with hot water only and even after submerging myself in the hot water, my shaking didn't subside. The water heater could not keep up with the heat I needed so Debbie boiled water to add to the bath. She looked worried and through my shaking I asked, "Is this all we can do? Should I go to the hospital? What did the doctor say?" She responded, "He said if you make it through the night I should bring you into the office."

It took me about six months to fully recover from Valley Fever during which I had little work and made a decision to fully immerse myself to market the moving and storage operations software I wrote...*The Movers Management System.* When we moved into the house just before Joseph was born, we rented our old one. We sold it to finance the business. Playing a role of a sales man was difficult for me but I learned that to make a sale one needed to be persistent. It took six months but I sold my first system to a local Allied Van Lines agent and as luck would have it, he was a member of the Allied Van Lines' Board of Directors. It is said most new businesses go out of business their first year. I was determined to last at least that long and when I was in the middle of the second year I asked for advice from my ex-employer Bob who was now a part-time investor. After we discussed my business plan and my current clients and prospects it was obvious to Bob that I lacked capital. He became my silent partner. In our fourth year of business and after we sold sixteen systems most were in Arizona but we also had installed systems in LA, Chicago, Buffalo, Tampa Bay, and even Newport, Rhode Island; we finally got the break we were waiting for...an invitation to the Allied Van Lines convention. What made it special was that it was a closed convention and if invited your company was a sanctioned vendor partner.

We did very well. The product demonstrations were well received and our pricing was very attractive. There were two other moving system vendors invited and essentially, corporate stated that since there are no plans to underwrite a standard computer system for their agents, the invited computer system vendors offered viable options. The Vice President of my biggest competitor whose office was located in Maryland kept prodding me to talk to him. Experience from other conventions taught me that he was very good in getting information that they used in competing with me. He did convince my sales manager to try to get me to talk with him. However, I didn't and weeks later I regretted it.

The convention was in late October and by December first we had sold six systems, our best year ever. I was now dealing with new issues like equipment procurement and adding staff until the word came from one of the customers we just sold a system to, that he was cancelling the order because Allied Van Lines corporate changed plans and said they would be offering computer systems to the agents. Four others also cancelled their orders but one called and said he thought we had the best system out there and that he was going to go ahead with the order. The company was in a dire position. Here we were a few days before Christmas and in crisis. Cash flow was all sucked up in equipment orders and because we concentrated on closing Allied agents there were no other orders in the pipeline. Bob and I discussed our options and decided to close the company right after Christmas. I sent the deposit check back to the one faithful potential client and canceled his order. I found out through my client who was on the board that my competitor from Maryland had sold their entire moving and storage software to Allied Van Lines because they could no longer compete on the open market. The board agreed to the purchase because their largest agents had my competitor's systems and they were concerned of not having continued support. In addition, later still I heard that the VP who pursued to have a conversation with me at Allied's convention wanted to talk about the possibility of his and my company merging.

The business closed. Losing a business that one creates and nurtures for years is a loss that is difficult to "let go" but before the end of the year, I became the Manager of Information Systems for one of my former clients. It became the longest employed job of my life. Bill and David are savvy business men with compassion towards the associates working with them. Through their method of managing a business, my true nature blossomed.

# Chapter 7

Being employed helped get back to basics. The hours spent to develop a business were staggering and my relationship with my family was reeling. I vowed that I would be the father I wanted to be. Only my children can answer whether I did or not. However, I learned more from my children than from anyone else.

The dry and warm climate of Arizona did help me deal with my arthritis symptoms. Even a little bit of physical exercise caused pain which to control I was ingesting 10-12 ibuprofen a day. One day I was talking with my brother-in-law about his back doctor while opening the day's mail and starting reading an advertisement postcard that asked, "Do you have these symptoms?" I had eight of the ten and right then decided that I would set up an appointment with the chiropractor smiling at me from that piece of mail. The initial examination consisted of having X-rays taken and a discussion of my symptoms. After review of the X-rays, the doctor asked if I have had a car accident a number of years ago. I told him that I did about 20 years past while I still worked for the bank in Chicago when I was coming home from an employee basketball game. It was raining and a car ran me off the side of the road and hit a tree totaling my car. The car that ran me off the road stopped about half a block down until I was able to pull myself out and saw it speed away. When this accident occurred, my dad was concerned and it was then I became aware of my dad's involvement with breaking up a theft ring at the freight company he was employed. He had contacted the FBI. Before there was enough evidence to arrest the people involved, he started getting threats about harm coming to his family and to reinforce the threat, they slashed his car's tires.

At was after three months of chiropractic treatment that Debbie noticed that I was not shuffling to the bathroom after getting out of bed. I no longer needed ibuprofen or any other medication to get through the day. Physical health aided me to begin expanding my mental and emotional health. After a lengthy search for religion before I was married, I rejected organized religions but still felt there was more than what our senses tell us. I again began research not just of Christian faiths but other beliefs ranging from Buddhism to agnosticism. This helped quiet my fears to get past an incident that involved my daughters and Debbie's older brother that shook my family's foundations and its eventual demise, as we knew it. Though we paid a heavy price for being unwilling participants, it did initiate a healing process for many people and prevented others being hurt as we had.

Everyday I would voice a mantra while driving to work, asking for the strength to recognize and do God's will. At that time, I wasn't sure what God meant to me. It definitely was not the God as in many organized religions where God is represented as Michelangelo's painting in the Sistine Chapel. My belief was evolving that God was not a "person-like" entity but more a compilation of everything in the universe. I believe that before we come into this world we accept a plan for our life; that we decide what we want to experience. When we wander away from our awareness objectives, change happens. It is how I became a victim of downsizing.

Bill and David's company profits were flat and when the discussion among the company's managers of what we would do to reduce cost, I volunteered that it would make sense to have me released. I was more of the expansion type of employee and if the company continued to be stagnant, my services would not be necessary. So after three years of not meeting profit goals, they took me at my word and released me, my only objection was that I was not included in the decision-making. I was again an independent consultant and took it in stride; deciding I would not become an employee again. The benefits of working from home far outweighed the uncertainty of not having a weekly paycheck. One of my contracts had me working with the County Attorney's office. It being a long-term contract my client's expectations of me were like being an employee. Again, everyday I would recite my mantra while driving to the office. One morning I awoke with a dream still vividly in my memory and told Debbie that I had a dream about a woman on the project team at work. She immediately became interested. I put her mind at ease telling her that the dream had me holding Lisa in my arms and consoling her and that we were wearing white robes as they wore in Roman times. About a month later, I was working on Saturday morning and was essentially alone, when that same dream-memory where I am holding Lisa overcame me. Only this time it continued past the consoling. Roman guards appeared and signaled us to rise and follow them down a dark corridor to a courtyard entrance. I broke out in a sweat became emotionally drained and went home.

Days later the project team planned a lunch but when the day came the only Lisa and I were still able to go. On our way back to the office, I asked if she believed in reincarnation and she asked, "Why?" I then told her about my dream-memory but did not include the emotional outbreak I had at the office. She took it seriously and said, "Maybe I do." We became friends and had lunch once or twice a week .I was driving to Costco when I again was overcome with a dream-memory that forced me to pull off and park the car. It was so powerful and consuming that it forced an emotional outburst from my innermost being. After this incident, my feelings about Lisa grew and I knew we were once together in a past time. I wrote my  memory down as a script because a dream-memory is many times like watching a movie. Here it is in screen-play form..

# Scene 01

FADE IN:

INTERIOR. DIRT FLOOR ROOM—LATE AFTERNOON
Stark room with whiffs of sand swirling from the high window.

I am holding Lisa, we are both draped in white linen robes. I stroke her hair.

ME
Peace... Peace... All will be well. (in Latin)

Two guards enter the room.

GUARD
It's your time. Stand!

Lisa and I manage weak smiles as we stand and turn toward the door.

INTERIOR. LONG DIMLY LIT CORRIDOR

We are led by the first guard, through a corridor lit only by the light from the entrance. As we approach the entrance, crowd sounds begin to swell.

Laughter blends with guttural screams, louder... louder...

The late afternoon sun comes pressing into the corridor, momentarily blinding, settling to a subdued haze of dust.

They stop less then ten steps from the entrance. We embrace.

EXTERIOR. HIGH ABOVE ARENA... A BIRD'S EYE VIEW

The crowd slowly becomes hushed...almost complete silence...then... WHOMP... WHOMP... WHOMP...the crowd roars at the sight of the beheadings.

EXTERIOR. CLOSING TO ARENA ACTIVITY

A rush of activity...the arena floor is cleared of the lifeless torsos.

EXTERIOR. CLOSE TO ACTIVITY IN ARENA

The heads, one with amazement still in the eyes, are placed on stakes and offered to the crowd for a more detail study.

INTERIOR. IN CORRIDOR

LISA
Is that our destiny?

ME
We will not be abandoned. The peace of Christ will sustain us.

LISA
The love we have will sustain us. Through all of time...

Lisa places her hand on my cheek.

The guard pulls on Lisa's hand and motions us to move into the arena.

EXTERIOR. ON THE ARENA FLOOR

Blood colored sand is kicked into the air as the guard pushes us onto the arena floor and past the beheading blocks.

The crowd cheers the new participants of entertainment.

Lisa and I are led to the strapping frame centered in the arena. They stop. They watch rope being tossed over the top. The crowd reacts to each action.

Guards approach us, and nearly simultaneously remove our robes, leaving us naked. We look into each other's eyes and keep our focus on each other.

Quickly, a guard grabs both of our right hands and ties them together, while another guard ties our right ankles together.

We are moved to directly under the strapping frame's upper beam, where three ropes are already dangling.

The ropes are tied to each of our left hands and the middle rope is pulled through the knot tying our right hands.

A tug on the ropes pulls us on our toes. Our left ankles are then tied to the supporting beams forming a double X with our bodies.

The guards who tied us leave. The crowd noise begins to swell as the executioner enters the arena. He looks at the audience and deliberately draws a six inch dagger and presents it for their approval.

He approaches and gently draws a shallow incision across my abdomen. Blood seeps out onto my loins and down my legs. He then duplicates the act with Lisa.

We have the slightest of a wince, never letting our eyes stray from each other.

The executioner bows and backs from the strapping frame with a flourish. The crowd reacts knowingly of the action to follow.

The first dog is released, crazed with hunger and abuse, foam surrounds his mouth. Quickly another dog is released, then another, and another...until there are six running along the perimeter of the arena, growling and biting at each other.

After circling the arena about three times, the guards sound a diversion as the dogs approach their station, sending the dogs to the center of the arena toward me and Lisa.

There was only two diversions before the first dog gets the scent of blood and races toward the strapping frame.

The beast quickly circles the prey. The other dogs are now on their way to join in the foray.

ME
The Christ is within us... We accept our fate. Join me Lisa... Let the beasts know
The Christ is here...

LISA and ME (in unison)
The Christ is within us...
The Christ is within us...
The Christ is within us...

Suddenly, the dogs stop, as if they lost the scent of their prey. They growl and bark...but soon they just move away.

The crowd is momentarily hushed...so unusual...they have been cheated...they begin a chant that was foreboding to the executioner.

INTERIOR. INSIDE THE MAIN ENTRANCE TO THE ARENA.

The executioner stands uneasy.

EXECUTIONER
Go slay the Christians!

The executioner pushes the closest guard into the arena.

The guard quickly draws his sword and advances toward the strapping frame.

Unexpectedly, the jaws of the first dog latches onto the back of the guard's neck. He falls trying to shake the canine free. By the time his knee touches the ground, the other five dogs are onto him tearing away flesh and limb.

The crowd roars with approval.

The captain of the guard motions to a platoon of archers in the stands, whereby the dogs are killed by a barrage of arrows.

Again the crowd reacts with approval.

The executioner, seeing the last dog die, again enters the arena, carrying the beheading cleaver.

He approaches the Christians slowly revolving the ax with fresh blood still on the edge over his head.

ME
The Christ within...do not forsake us.

LISA
Please don't let us die...

ME
Lisa I promise to be with you forever...we will be saved for the Christ is within us...
I love you...

As the executioner is within a step from the Christians, our heads bow, and bodies go limp.

He stops and bends to see my face...and moves slowly until he is upon us. He pulls my head back by my hair... I am lifeless.

EXTERIOR. MOVING RAPIDLY UPWARD FROM THE ARENA UNTIL THE ARENA IS OBSCURED BY THE CLOUDS.

# Chapter 8

Debbie was suggesting we divorce while we were shopping for a desk that Joseph would use. I suggested we try counseling again and then we let the subject drop. Divorce was never an option. Yes, we were going through unhappy times where my share of the cause was searching for who I was which left me moody and introspective. One night during a meaningless argument between Debbie and I, she asked "What do you want from me?" I responded, "I would like to have a relationship with you as I have with Lisa." That was all I could say before she left the house and stayed with friends. I tried to explain that Lisa and I had an effortless exchange of thoughts and ideas. I wanted to assure her that Lisa and I were not having an affair; we displayed affection but never remotely anything sexual, not even a kiss. However, unfortunately, a mind set took place and there would be no option but divorce. We amicably agreed to asset distribution and I would handle filing the paperwork while I lived with my mother. Two months later after I returned from my older brother's memorial service and a couple of attempts to perhaps get together again with Debbie, I filed the paperwork which would take about ten weeks to process since it was an uncontested divorce. A month later, I found my mother on the floor unable to stand up. I got her into my car and drove her to the emergency care center. She had a stroke.

About two weeks before Debbie's and my divorce would be finalized, I was in my mom's room at the recovery therapy center when in walked a very attractive dark haired nurse and was startled to see me there. She asked, "Is this Anne's room?" I responded, "Yes, she's in therapy right now." She smiled and said, "I'll be back later." When my mom returned to her room, I told her about the nurse coming in her room and that I thought she was very attractive. Quickly my mom said, "Well, ask her out on a date." I laughed, "First of all I've forgotten how to ask for a date and secondly, I'm not sure if I'm ready for dating." The next day, I was to take my mom home. Other than having to walk with a cane, my mom was back to normal. When I left there to bring my mom home there was a twinge of hope that I would see that nurse again and maybe ask her out but there was no sign of her. As I walked into my mom's room, she asked, "Is Susan out there?" "Who's Susan" I replied. "She's the nurse you thought was cute" and she went on about talking with her and asking her questions like if she was married or dating anyone and if she thought her son was cute and if she minded giving her phone number so her son could call her. Before even kissing her hello, here was my matchmaking mom handing me a slip of paper with a phone number on it. For the next couple of days, my mother would be asking "Did you call her yet?" followed by "Give Susan a call." The first try I got a busy signal, the second no answer but on the third, there was a "Hello." I felt like I was in high school again. We agreed to meet for dinner that Saturday at a place where she once worked as a cook. That Saturday as I went out the front door, my girls were sitting on the porch and noticing that I was visibly nervous they assured me that everything would be OK.

I waited outside of the restaurant trying to remember to be myself when around the corner, came Susan, a Julia Roberts look-a-like. She was more beautiful now then when I first saw her. We talked throughout the meal and I felt as comfortable as I can be. There was no pretense from either of us. I found out that she had a four year old daughter which caused a flashback of a dream I had a few weeks ago when I was telling my kids that I will probably never be with anyone again for "Who would want me?" In my dream if you haven't guessed by now was a beautiful dark haired woman with a daughter. It was one of those dreams that you want to go back to sleep to continue it. We dated and by next spring, we married.

I was in the best shape since coming out of boot camp. I was hiking at least four times a week and eating healthy where I consulted with my inner being. I had steady consulting work that I contributed to my pursuit of "who am I", "what do I believe", and "who is God and how does he relate to my world." My consulting work was beginning to evolve to be more mentoring of staff in methods of teamwork rather than just programming analyst work. My IT Team Coach newsletter that presented my method of leading a project team was being well received. I was being quoted in trade magazine articles and even had my own articles published in trade journals.

My only fear was, was I moving too fast. Susan and I were waiting for the plane to Denver to begin loading. I was going to a convention where many "New Age" leaders were to be speaking. Susan and my mom being Christians and not knowing much about alternative religions felt it was a cult and let their disapproval be known to me. When the flight was delayed for the second time, I got up and said to Susan, "Let's go home." From this point on, things started to become more challenging. Coaching work was limited and I took more programming/analyst work and eventually took loans to pay the bills.

While I had consulting work in Tucson I would pass by the signs on the freeway south of Phoenix luring one to visit the casino and often thought to take a break and have some fun. When I was near the end of my contract, I gave in to the signs and turned off the freeway and into the casino. It would be the first time I went alone. Up to then, I would take my mom to the local casinos for a couple of hours. After giving in that first time, I eventually found myself at the casino a lot. When working for a company in Scottsdale I would go for lunch and end up at the casino, sometimes returning late to work but I resisted going in the evenings. There was still some control of the amount of money used for gambling but it was slowly slipping away. I don't know when I became a pathological gambler.

# CHAPTER 9

Definitions that could be in a dictionary:

Addiction: Compulsive physiological need for a habit-forming substance or activity.

Addict: To devote or give (oneself) habitually or compulsively.

A dictionary has no idea what an addiction is, only addicts do. It is when all other reality moves to a state that cannot be focused on. An addict struggles knowing that all the other things happening are of more importance yet the only reality an addict knows is the addiction that controls the addict's life. At my first Gamblers Anonymous (GA) meeting I attended, the moderator stated, a compulsive gambler has three futures: 1) insanity, 2) incarceration, or 3) suicide. I have experience with number one and three.

Of all the challenges I faced this is the hardest. However, my addiction is also my greatest gift. I'll explain but first I want to share the wonderful events that occurred while under the influence of my addiction. The births of my grandchildren, Aurora, Evie and Oliver, my daughters wedding, my son's graduation from college, my son's pursuit of his music career, my oldest daughter's continued growth as an artist that captures many people's memories as the photos in this book has, my step-daughter's academic accomplishments and many more that passed over me without the acknowledgement and support that was warranted.

My spiral into pathological gambling was secured with all night casino stays. I would find myself coming home not believing what just occurred. After the first time, I voiced my first vow that it would never happen again. But it did...and then again...and again. During this state of insanity, I literally could not leave the casino. In my head, I would hear arguments of staying and leaving. There were times when I had no money left to gamble but still wandered around the casino for hours. When finally I would leave, thoughts of suicide immediately took control. Shame and disbelief of my actions immersed every aspect of my being. I wanted it to stop. Each time I stayed longer at the casino then  what would be considered acceptable, my mind drifted to a method to get through this hopeless situation. I felt I reached bottom every time this happened.

I sold the house and Susan and I got apartments in the same complex. I still held out that I could rid myself of this addiction. After quickly losing all the proceeds form the sale of my home for 25 years, I was resolute that the only way to resolve my addiction was through death. This came about when, after another all-nighter where thoughts of suicide filled my consciousness, I heard the voice that assured me that I would recover from last night's ordeal.

I spoke aloud and asked, "Where are you when the other voice tempts me to go to the casino?" There was a slight delay before hearing, "I AM the same." It didn't take long before I realized that my insanity of hearing a voice in my head when I was pursuing ideas to improve teamwork now extended to hearing voices that completely controlled me. I accepted that the inner voice was of divine nature—of God or perhaps *Elijah.* I asked but did not receive confirmation.

I attended my daughters wedding in Scotland through the generosity of my mom. When I returned home, the money that should have paid my mother back was "delivered" to the casino by my addiction. It was time. All my life insurance was in force and it would be the only way to provide a future for my family. As I looked at the codeine tablets, I came to task of what exactly I was going to do. It was the only way in my mind to finally stop my insanity and yet provide for my family. My suicide attempt was unsuccessful. After a few days of being seriously ill, I found myself thinking that maybe there was another solution. I began looking for work on-line, sending a minimum of 50 resumes a week. I had not paid my rent and expected eviction proceedings any day. September came and went and my 50 resumes a week went out without any acknowledgement and soon October came and went along with my resumes and still no eviction. In November, I received the anticipated eviction notice. I remember telling my daughter that it was in God's hand and I had to believe that "whatever happens was meant to be."

The week before Thanksgiving, I had a response to a sent resume. I went to the staffing company for an interview and the next day I received a phone call asking me to meet with the company interested in hiring me. The interview was amazing. Terry, a beautiful woman and the executive director of the organization I was interviewing with, presented the job as projects to be scheduled. It was if I was already hired. Finally, I asked, "When do you want me to start?" "Is Monday OK?" she responded. I was on cloud nine coming home. I finally got a job and knew I would be a good fit. I parked my car and as I approached my apartment, I saw two people going up the stairs; one was the maintenance person and the other a sheriff deputy. They were at my apartment and I got their attention. They said they didn't want any trouble but I was being evicted and I would have about 15 minutes to get anything I needed before they changed the locks. The best of days turned to the worst of days. I gathered some clothes and personal items and went to put them in my car. I then went to Susan's apartment and stayed there for a while until she told me she would have nothing to do with me again. I left and on my way to my car, two Jehovah's Witness disciples confronted me. They noticed I was troubled and wanted to help. They began with the premise that they had the answer but to my amazement, I stayed my course and essentially told them that my trouble was God given and that I appreciated what I was going through. I explained that all things are of God that there was no separation. All things are of God. After about 10 minutes, they sensed that they had no valid argument against my belief of God. I left and experienced the event cited in Chapter 1.

It was the warrior, Ollie that came through for me. His conviction that I was worth supporting pulled me through by paying my past due rents and the next month's rent. I had another chance. As I was coming down the mountain I accepted that I would write what needed to be written as I assimilated the knowledge that was transferred to me.

The first day on my job, I met another past soul. Shanda was the person I was replacing. She contracted for a number of weeks after leaving the company to help me become acclimated with what she did as an employee. Her energy and insight helped pulled me from despair and again made me a productive being. To this day, I do not believe she knows the influence she made on my life.

One would think that an incident that I experienced as in Chapter 1 would bring one to changing their ways. It didn't. I wrote the first chapter and toiled with additional chapters, to no success. I continued to struggle with my addiction.

I wanted to know what kind of addiction I was dealing with and asked my inner voice to lead me to a better understanding of what I was going through. Then while taking a summer afternoon nap, what I asked for happened. I had a dream and wrote it down so I would not forget it.

*I was in a room of a casino hotel where I left and went to the casino floor and sat at a table but I forgot something, I don't know what it was but it was necessary. I looked in all my pockets and thought I must have laid it down somewhere so I left the table and went from area to area in the casino looking for this thing. Finally a casino "boss" came and asked me by name if everything was all right. I told him I was looking for this thing and he assured me it was most likely in my room. I went to my room and decided to leave so I started packing. I kept on packing until my suitcase was full and yet there were a lot more things in the room that were mine, some of the things were things from the past. Things my kids gave me or made for me, like painted rocks and pictures in a homemade frame. I started to worry about how I was to take everything out of the room but kept up the packing until I heard voices behind me. I thought that the women in the room were to have it after I left. They were happy and having an on-going conversation. I finally turned to ask the two women if they had seen what I was looking for. They shook their heads no and then asked where was I from. I said, "Chicago originally" and noticed that one of the women was really pretty and I felt I would like to ask her out when she said, "I know a doctor Coker there, do you know him?" I said I did not and she said, "Well if you go back you should look him up".*

I woke up and almost instantly knew that this was important. So I looked up "coker:" on google, narrowed it down with "doctor" and again with "Chicago" and finally "gambling" when the first item appeared:

> Books Received—Journal of Health Politics, Policy and Law 25:6
> Pathological Gambling: The Making of a Medical Problem. Brian Castellani...
> Richard J. **Coker**. New York: St. Martin's, 2000. 279 pp. $27.95 cloth...
> muse.jhu.edu/journals/journal_of_health_politics_policy_and_law/v025/25.6books_received.html

I looked up the availability of the book reviewed by Dr. Coker in the Phoenix library. The central branch had it and I immediately went to get it.

Castellani's book gave me insight of the clinical diagnosis of my addiction but I knew better or at least my insanity knew better. Since God gave me this for a reason, though I have no inkling of why, I knew that following the path would lead to the "white rabbit".

To cover gambling losses I took payday loans to pay rent and other necessities. Before long, my payday loan payments exceeded my pay. When this occurrence first came about, I withdrew my pay before the payday loan payments came through which was around 12:30 AM, and gambled. I won enough to cover my debts. When next payday came I did the same thing, only I lost. Only I lost everything, which brings me to today. I can't pay my rent and my "payday loan" people are getting very anxious.

I voiced that I did not want to live my life as it is. I want my addiction to end and if that means the "final end", so be it. I asked to end it, I heard…finish what you agreed to, and your life will change. Upon waking Sunday morning, I felt it would be my last day. The next day, I began writing what should be written. It is now Saturday night and what should be written…is.

# CHAPTER 10

My trip down the mountain confirmed many of the ideas and beliefs I now know.

The substantiation came as passages in the King James Version bible.

They are:

Luke 17.21

"Neither shall they say, lo here! or, lo there! for behold, **the kingdom of God is within you**"

*Who are we? Now know we are children of God.*

Mark 12.

28 And one of the scribes came, and having heard them reasoning together, and perceiving that he had answered them well, asked him, Which is the first commandment of all?

29 And Jesus answered him, The first of all the commandments is, Hear, O Israel; The Lord our God is one Lord:

30 And thou shalt love the Lord thy God with all thy heart, and with all thy soul, and with all thy mind, and with all thy strength: this is the first commandment.

31 And the second is like, namely this, **Thou shalt love thy neighbour as thyself**. There is none other commandment greater than these.

32 And the scribe said unto him, Well, Master, thou hast said the truth: for there is one God; and there is none other but he:

33 And to love him with all the heart, and with all the understanding, and with all the soul, and with all the strength, and to love his neighbour as himself, is more than all whole burnt offerings and sacrifices.

*Who are we? Now know we are children of God.*

John 14.

10 Believest thou not that I am in the Father, and the Father in me? the words that I speak unto you I speak not of myself: but the Father that dwelleth in me, he doeth the works.

11 Believe me that I am in the Father, and the Father in me: or else believe me for the very works' sake.

12 Verily, verily, I say unto you, He that believeth on me, **the works that I do shall he do also; and greater works than these shall he do**; because I go unto my Father.

13 And whatsoever ye shall ask in my name, that will I do, that the Father may be glorified in the Son.

14 If ye shall ask any thing in my name, I will do it.

*Who are we? Now know we are children of God.*

John 15.

12 **This is my commandment, That ye love one another, as I have loved you.**

13 **Greater love hath no man than this, that a man lay down his life for his friends**.

*Who are we? Now know we are children of God.*

OK, my end of our agreement is done. God, it's your move.

# CHAPTER 11

It is 5 weeks since writing what is "to be written". I emailed copies to my four children the day after finishing the last chapter. A few days later, I emailed my story to my siblings and closest friends telling them that I wrote this as a legacy for my children. My sister, Sharon, read my story the day after Easter and responded with the following.

*"This needs to be published... I really don't know how to do that, but I know in my heart this needs to be published. Yes for your kids, but also for others who struggle with the same demons you struggle with, and for hope. I think this goes under the heading of inspired writing...submit it!"*

A few days later, I prayed that if my story is to be published then direct me to a publisher. Early Sunday morning two weeks after Easter Sunday, I googled "publishers". I went to the first publisher on the list and requested permission to send my manuscript to them. Three days later on Thursday, I received an email requesting my bio and a formatted copy of "Now Know". The following Monday, "Now Know" was accepted for publication.

Has my life changed since having done what I was meant to do? Yes.

Are challenges still presented that test my very essence? Yes.

To meet my challenges, I ask the following questions.

Does God exist?

Is God omnipotent?

Is God love?

Can evil exist where there is love?

I now know that I am a child of God...and so are you.

Godspeed.